I CAN COUNT TO TEN AND BACK AGAIN

By Linda Hayward
Illustrated by Maggie Swanson

A SESAME STREET/GOLDEN PRESS BOOK

Published by Western Publishing Company, Inc.,
in conjunction with Children's Television Workshop.

Library of Congress Catalog Card Number: 80-50848 ISBN: 0-307-23116-X

One day Big Bird decided to set up a store on
Sesame Street. His store had a counter, a cash register, a
telephone, and a scale. There were plenty of shelves, too.
He needed shelves to hold the things that would be for sale.
All he needed now were some things to sell.

Big Bird poured water into a glass.

"I want to sell things that my friends on Sesame Street will want," said Big Bird. "Someone always wants a glass of water."

He put the glass of water on the shelf.

Now he had ONE glass of water for sale.

Big Bird found two little wheels on Sesame Street.
"I should have unusual things for sale," said Big Bird.
"What if someone comes to my store and wants to buy
two wheels?"
He put the wheels on the shelf.
Now he had TWO little wheels for sale.

Big Bird went to the vegetable garden and pulled three carrots out of the ground.

"I should have some snacks for sale," said Big Bird. "A fresh carrot is a good snack."

He put the carrots on the shelf.

Now he had THREE carrots for sale.

Big Bird drew four pictures of himself.
"Someone might want to buy a picture to hang on the wall," said Big Bird. "A picture is a nice decoration."
He put the pictures on the shelf.
Now he had FOUR Big Bird pictures for sale.

Big Bird found five empty ketchup bottles.
"You never know when someone is going to want to buy five empty ketchup bottles," thought Big Bird.
He put the bottles on the shelf.
Now he had FIVE empty ketchup bottles for sale.

Big Bird baked six chocolate chip peanut butter cookies.
"I know someone on Sesame Street who loves cookies,"
said Big Bird. "I will sell these cookies to him."
Big Bird put the cookies on the shelf.
Now he had SIX chocolate chip peanut butter cookies
for sale.

Big Bird received seven wax bananas in the mail.

"I know someone on Sesame Street who collects wax bananas," said Big Bird.

He put the wax bananas on the shelf.

Now he had SEVEN wax bananas for sale.

Big Bird found eight rotten eggs.

"Nobody wants to buy rotten eggs," said Big Bird. "But I will leave them on the shelf for now and throw them away later."

He put the eggs on the shelf.

Now he had EIGHT rotten eggs to throw away later.

Big Bird made nine noisy rattles.
"Oscar the Grouch loves to make noise," said Big Bird.
"I should have something for him to buy."
Big Bird put the rattles on the shelf.
Now he had NINE noisy rattles for sale.

Big Bird found ten used golf balls in the park.

"I will never, never, never be able to sell ten used golf balls," said Big Bird. "So I will put them on the bottom shelf where they won't get in my way."

Big Bird put the golf balls on the bottom shelf.

Now he had TEN used golf balls that he would never sell.

At last Big Bird's store was full of things for sale.

He had ONE glass of water, TWO little wheels, THREE carrots, FOUR Big Bird pictures, FIVE empty ketchup bottles, SIX chocolate chip peanut butter cookies, SEVEN wax bananas, EIGHT rotten eggs to throw away later, NINE noisy rattles, and TEN used golf balls.

One, two, three, four, five, six, seven, eight, nine, ten.

All he needed now were some customers.

Bert came by Big Bird's store. He was wearing his golf
hat and his golf shoes. He was carrying his golf bag filled
with golf clubs.

"Gee, Bert," said Big Bird. "You look like a customer
who would like to buy an empty ketchup bottle."

"No," said Bert. "I would like to buy golf balls."

Big Bird sold the ten used golf balls to Bert.

Prairie Dawn came by Big Bird's store.

"I would like to buy those nine noisy rattles," she said.

"Do you plan to make a lot of noise?" asked Big Bird.

"No," said Prairie Dawn. "I plan to buy those rattles before Oscar buys them. I hate noise!"

Big Bird sold the NINE noisy rattles to Prairie Dawn.

"By the way," said Prairie Dawn, "what is that awful rotten egg smell?"

Oscar the Grouch came by Big Bird's store.

"I couldn't help but notice the wonderful smell coming from your store," he said. "Do you by chance have rotten eggs for sale?"

Big Bird sold the EIGHT rotten eggs to Oscar.

The Count was Big Bird's next customer.

"Greetings!" cried the Count. "I am so happy because I see you have exactly what I have always wanted. For years now I have been counting parties, parades, thunderstorms, kittens, snowflakes, birthday cakes. Just once I'd like to count wax bananas!"

Big Bird was able to sell the SEVEN wax bananas to the Count.

Then Cookie Monster came by. He was hungry, as usual.

"Do you have six heads of lettuçe?" asked Cookie Monster.

"No," said Big Bird.

"Do you have six stalks of celery?" asked Cookie Monster.

"No," said Big Bird. "But I have six chocolate chip peanut butter cookies."

"COWABUNGA!" cried Cookie.

Big Bird sold the SIX chocolate chip peanut butter cookies to Cookie Monster.

A few minutes later, Big Bird sold the FIVE empty
ketchup bottles to Sherlock Hemlock.

"Gee, Mr. Hemlock," said Big Bird, "why do you need
five empty ketchup bottles?"

"That is easy," explained Sherlock Hemlock. "As the
world's greatest detective, I intend to solve the mystery of
the missing ketchup."

Granny Bird came to see Big Bird's store.

"I like your store, Big Bird," she said. "I like the sign you made, too. I especially like those four pictures you drew of yourself. Are they for sale?"

"Not anymore," said Big Bird. "I am going to give them to you."

Big Bird gave the FOUR Big Bird pictures to Granny Bird.

The Amazing Mumford came by and did a magic trick.
He pulled three rabbits out of his hat.
   Big Bird took three carrots off his shelf.
   "Here is a carrot for each rabbit," said Big Bird.
   He gave the THREE carrots to the Amazing Mumford.

Big Bird was beginning to wonder if anyone was going to buy the two wheels when Grover came by pulling his toy airplane. The toy airplane was missing something.

"I am so sad because my airplane is missing its cute little wheels," said Grover. "Have you seen them?"

"I have just what you need," said Big Bird.

He gave the TWO little wheels to Grover.

Now Big Bird had nothing left in his store but the glass of water.

"I guess no one on Sesame Street wanted a glass of water today."

Just then Oscar's pet worm Slimey appeared.

"Do you sell swimming pools?" he asked Big Bird.

"No," said Big Bird. "All I have left to sell is this one glass of water."

"Great!" cried Slimey. "That's just the right size swimming pool for me. I'll take it!"

Once again Big Bird had nothing for sale. His shelves were empty.

He had sold or given away TEN used golf balls, NINE noisy rattles, EIGHT rotten eggs, SEVEN wax bananas, SIX chocolate chip peanut butter cookies, FIVE empty ketchup bottles, FOUR Big Bird pictures, THREE carrots, TWO little wheels, and ONE glass of water.

Ten, nine, eight, seven, six, five, four, three, two, one! Count to ten and back again!